PERSONALITY PROFILES

Handwriting Analysis

What your handwriting says about you!

K.J. Davies

Illustrated by *Amie McIntyre*
Edited by *Thea Feldman*

B Plus Marketing, Inc.
765 Silversmith Circle, Lake Mary, FL 32746

To Amie, Mark, Thea, Ken and Marie —
Thanks for your support!

ISBN 1-931623-06-6

Published by B Plus Books
765 Silversmith Circle, Lake Mary, FL 32746

Printed in USA.

Cover Design by Amie McIntyre
Illustrations by Amie McIntyre

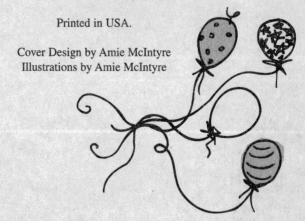

Contents

Chapter One
Handwriting: What's Write About You!

How many times a day do you write something down? Take a minute and think. You write a lot while you're in school — copying things from the blackboard, writing papers in class, and oh yeah, even passing that note to your friend. At home you probably write at least part of your homework. And, if you make lists of friends to call, leave a note for your mom, or keep a journal, then you write even more.

If you're like most people, you probably never even think about the actual act of writing. Since you learned how to write in cursive, otherwise known as "script," you probably just scribble away and then pray you can read what you've written! Your focus is on the content of what you've written, not on the physical form of the actual letters.

Well, did you know that the actual way that you write — make your letters — can reveal a lot about your personality? It's true. Your handwriting provides tons of clues to who you really are.

For nearly a century now, people have been studying other people's handwriting to learn about the personality of the writers. The science known as graphology reveals personality traits and tendencies based on handwriting analysis. Because your handwriting is something you do automatically, it is really a "graph" of the workings of your mind as much as a way to communicate and express information about any and everything else in the whole world.

That's right — to the trained eye, your handwriting makes your personality an open book. Sounds weird? Well, grab a piece of paper (plain paper - no lines on it) and write down a paragraph or two in your normal writing style. In this case the content of what you write won't matter at all, so just let it all hang out. Write about what you did today or what you want to do this weekend. Write about what you want to do with your friends. Write something about your brother or sister or mom, dad, or even your goldfish! Focus on what you're writing about — not on the writing itself. Then sign your full name.

You're going to learn how to analyze your own handwriting during the course of this book. By the time you're done, you'll have a better understanding of who you are and how your handwriting supports that. So keep that piece of paper handy. You'll need it as you read on, in order to build your own personality profile.

By the time you're done with this book you'll not only know more about yourself, you'll also be able to figure out the personality traits of other people. All you'll need is some handwriting samples. Check out these signatures from some of today's biggest stars. Refer back to them as you go through the book and see if you can build personality profiles for Britney Spears, Jennifer Lopez, Jim Carrey, Wayne Gretzky, Jessica Simpson and N'Sync. The last chapter of this book analyzes their signatures — but don't peek! It'll be more fun if you wait and see how close you get.

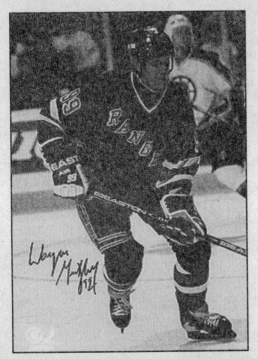

 Okay, ready... set... reveal!

Chapter Two

Building Your Emotional Base: That's Deeply Intense!

Remember the last time you and your friends went to the movies? How easily did you feel like screaming at the scary parts or laughing or crying? How strongly did you feel those things? Did those feelings linger, or did they fade pretty quickly as the movie went on?

How easily you feel things shows how emotionally responsive you are. How long those feelings last shows how deeply you feel things. Taken together these two traits form part of your emotional base. There's no good or bad to this; it's just part of who you are.

You can actually find out about your emotional base by looking at your handwriting. So be sure to have your handwriting sample with you now. The slant of your writing shows your responsiveness and the pressure you used to do the writing reveals your intensity. And once you know what to look for, there'll be no hiding it from you in anyone's handwriting. Think pretty intense? Well, you're about to be able to prove it!

Slant in Handwriting: Emotional Response

Very few people have truly a consistent slant in their handwriting. Most often there are some changes in the slant. But when you look at your own handwriting, you'll see a tendency for it to go either to the right, be straight up and down, or be a mix of the first two. The slant will reveal how you feel inside. It won't tell, all by itself, how you actually express what you feel to others. There are other traits in your handwriting that will show you that, and you'll see those a little later.

To get a good idea of the slant in your handwriting, check out the strokes in your writing. Lines or strokes in your handwriting that go up are called upstrokes. Lines that go down are called downstrokes. It's easy to figure out which are which — just think about how you made each letter. Which line did you write from bottom to top, and which line did you write from top to bottom? The part or line of a letter that you made from bottom to top is an upstroke.

Check out a lower case "l": The first stroke or line that you make in the letter is the upstroke; then you make the second line or stroke from the top of that upstroke down to the bottom. That's a downstroke.

To discover the slant in your handwriting (your emotional responsiveness), you need to pay attention to how you made the upstrokes in your writing sample. The angle is made from the bottom or beginning point of the upstroke to the top or ending point of the upstroke. Try and match your sample with one of the examples and samples that follow.

Right Slant:

extreme right

If you have a strong slant to the right in your handwriting, then you're a person who is very quick to respond emotionally to people or circumstances. You may experience a powerful emotional response in a situation where others may feel little or no emotional response. You have strong feelings a lot of the time.

Straight up Slant:

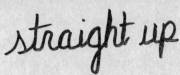

A person who is very slow to respond emotionally to people or circumstances has upstrokes in their handwriting that mostly go straight up. Where a right-slanter feels strong emotions in certain situations, the straight-up slanter may not feel anything in particular. The straight up slanter is a person who doesn't usually have strong feelings.

Mixed Slant:

mixed slant

When you see a real mix of slants, from straight up to extreme right, in the same handwriting, that's a sign of a person who doesn't have consistent emotional responses. That person may respond emotionally to some people and circumstances, and hardly respond at all to other people and circumstances. In some instances, this person has strong feelings, and in other instances they hardly have any feelings at all.

Which one of these three slants best describes you? How about the celebrities from the last chapter? Where did they come out in terms of their slant? How emotionally responsive are they?

There's a fourth type of slant - the left or back slant — which occurs very rarely, but is still worth mentioning, even though you'll probably

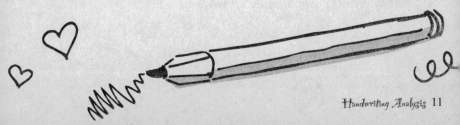

never see it. It's not the same as handwriting that just looks back slanted. The writing of some lefties can look really back slanted but the upstrokes in the writing are usually not left-slanted at all when compared to the rest of the writing. When the upstrokes themselves are really slanted to the left, this is a sign of a person who has probably had some really bad things happen to them; as a result, they want to stop responding emotionally. Something happened to make this person not want to feel emotions at all.

Pressure in Handwriting: Emotional Depth

Ever feel pressured when you write? Well, bet you never thought about the physical amount of pressure you use when doing it. The amount of pressure you apply to the pen and paper when you write reveals how deeply you feel things. Check out the three basic categories of writing pressure below. In the same way that you don't always slant your writing consistently, you're not always applying the same amount of pressure when you write. And, there are many more degrees of pressure that can be applied when pen touches paper than those listed below. You should find, however, that you fall mostly into one of the big three.

The amount of pressure in your handwriting also shows how strongly you are affected by your five senses. How deeply you respond to color, taste, sound, touch, and smell is also revealed by the amount of pressure you use in your writing.

Heavy Pressure:

heavy pressure ✵

Using a lot of pressure in writing - almost as though you're pushing the pen through the paper - reveals great emotional depth. Emotions play a very powerful role in your life and do not pass quickly. You'll also find yourself powerfully affected by your senses.

Moderate (Medium) Pressure:

✫ *moderate*

If you show medium pressure in your writing, then you're a person who is affected to a fair degree by your emotions, but not to the same degree as a writer who uses heavy pressure. Your emotions also pass/fade more quickly than those of the person who writes with a heavy pressure. You're also affected by your senses but to a lesser degree than someone who writes with a heavy pressure.

Light Pressure:

light pressure

Now let's consider someone whose writing touch is very light, who uses just barely enough pressure to get ink on the paper. This person is hardly affected at all emotionally for any length of time. Whatever emotions this person experiences pass quickly and have very little lasting effect. Similarly, the role of the senses in affecting this person is not very strong.

So, what does your handwriting reveal about your emotional depth and your senses? How deep did you find Jennifer Lopez to be? How strongly is Jim Carrey affected by his senses? Are you going to dwell on this for a while or are you ready to move on?!

Response and Depth Together:

Do you like to mix and match things — Outfits? Parts of a meal? How about personality traits?! Well, there are many different combos of level of responsiveness and degree of emotional depth that you can get in handwriting analysis. They're listed below. As you go through the possible combinations be on the lookout for the one that best describes your writing sample. Think about the celebrity writing samples too, and see what you come up with.

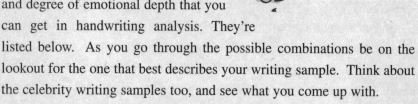

Extreme Response (Extreme Right Slant) &
Extreme Depth (Heavy Pressure):

extreme right

You're very quick to feel a strong emotional response to people and situations, and are deeply affected by those responses for a very long time.

Moderate Response (Moderate Right Slant) &
Extreme Depth (Heavy Pressure):

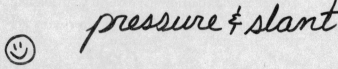

Your emotions can be fairly easily aroused. Once those emotions are aroused, you're deeply affected by them for a long time.

Low Response (Straight-up Slant) &
Extreme Depth (Heavy Pressure):

straight up

People or circumstances will not easily arouse your emotions - you remain emotionally "cool" inside, except, in the most extreme circumstances. When finally aroused, you're deeply affected by your emotions for a long time.

No Response (Extreme Left, or Back, Slant):

back slant

This is the rare person who has felt the need to "deaden" their emotions, to feel no real response even to extreme situations where others would respond very strongly.

Extreme Response (Extreme Right Slant) &
Moderate Depth (Moderate Pressure):

pressure & slant

You're very quick to feel a strong emotional response to people and situations, and are affected by those responses, but not a lot or for too long a time.

Moderate Response (Moderate Right Slant) &
Moderate Depth (Moderate Pressure):

pressure & slant

Your emotions are not too easily aroused. You're not too deeply affected or affected for too long a time once your emotions are aroused

Low Response (Straight-up Slant) &
Moderate Depth (Moderate Pressure):

straight up

Your emotions are hardly ever aroused by people or circumstances — you remain emotionally "cool" inside, except in extreme circumstances; and, even then, you're not deeply affected .

Extreme Response (Extreme
Right Slant) & Light Depth (Light Pressure):

pressure & slant

You're very quick to feel a strong emotional response to people and situations, but are hardly affected by those responses afterward. You forget your emotions as quickly as you feel them.

☆ ☆

Moderate Response (Moderate Right Slant) & Light Depth (Light Pressure):

pressure & slant

You're not too quick to feel a strong emotional response to people and situations. When aroused, you will not be much affected by those emotions afterward. You may forget them more quickly than you felt them.

Low Response (Straight-up Slant) & Light Depth (Light Pressure):

straight up

People or circumstances will only occasionally arouse the emotions of this person. This person will remain emotionally "cool" inside, except in extreme or special circumstances. When finally aroused, this person will not be long affected by those emotions, which are forgotten almost immediately.

Varied Response (Mixed Slant):

mixed slant

You've already seen that a person with a mixed slant handwriting will sometimes respond to people and circumstances and sometimes will not. The degree of pressure in the handwriting of this type of writer tells you the depth of emotions carried when there is a response.

Did you see yourself in any of the above combinations? Your handwriting might actually be a combination of combos. What about Wayne Gretzky or any of the other celebrities? Which combinations best describes their handwriting samples?

Chapter Three

Just Think About It!

Here's something else for you to think about. How do you go about solving problems? What kind of thinking do you use? Check out the following and see which of the three different approaches best describes what you would do.

Lisa, Jasmine and Trevor belong to a hiking club. They're out hiking one day when they wind up getting a little bit ahead of the rest of the group. They come across a footbridge that is the only way to cross a river gorge. The bridge is made of rope with wooden slats to walk on. The three friends know not to cross this bridge without the leader and the rest of the club, but they wonder if it'll be safe to cross the bridge at all. While they wait for the leader and the rest of the group to show up, they decide to take a crack at figuring out whether they'll eventually all be turning around or going across that bridge.

Jasmine steps forward first, and considers the situation. The wood slats don't appear to be cracked. Only a few of them are missing. The air is fairly calm - there's no wind to sway the bridge. Plus, the ropes don't appear to be frayed; they look well fastened, at least on this side of the river. Jasmine concludes that it will probably be safe for the group to go across.

Trevor isn't entirely convinced by Jasmine's reasoning. He finds some sizable rocks nearby and manages to roll several of them onto the footbridge. Figuring the weight to be enough of a test of the bridge, Trevor, too, decides that the bridge will be safe to cross.

Analytical Investigative

Lisa listens to Jasmine's reasoning and watches as Trevor tests the bridge with his rocks. Lisa, too, decides it will be safe to cross that bridge, basing her decision on all of the information she was able to gather from the other two.

When the rest of the hiking group shows up just minutes later, they neither turn around nor go across the bridge. Why? It was time for lunch of course! First they ate, then they went across single file and safely.

Would you most likely be Jasmine, Trevor, or Lisa in the above? Each one of them represents a different thinking style and approach to solving problematic situations.

Jasmine is an analytical thinker. She gathers information, thinks about the nature and the value of the information, and takes into account a lot of details in the process of reaching a conclusion. Jasmine looks to see how one thing relates to the other.

Trevor is an investigative thinker. He's not comfortable simply collecting facts and accepting them at face value. He needs to test his information before he accepts it. That's why he rolls rocks onto the bridge.

Lisa is a cumulative thinker. She's happiest when she gathers enough facts, one by one — without much testing — until she feels that all of the important facts or information are in place. A cumulative thinker like Lisa never jumps to conclusions. She prefers a slow, step-by-step walk — especially if it's across a bridge!

Of course there are many different ways to approach thinking and problem solving, but these three basic types can easily be revealed in your handwriting.

Analytical Thinking

The presence of downward-pointing wedges in letter formations (especially "m", "n", "h") is a sign of an analytical thinker.

Investigative Thinking

Upward-pointed wedges in letter formations (especially "m", "n", "h") indicate an investigative thinker.

Cumulative Thinking

m n h r

Broad "r" tops and very rounded tops on "m", "n" and "h" letters are a good sign that a cumulative thinker is around.

Sometimes more than one type can be found in the same handwriting, though one type may be more apparent than another.

Based on your handwriting sample, which type of thinker best describes you? How about your Mom? And what do you (and she) think about that?!

Chapter Four

Personality Plus —
Have a Personality Profile Party!

What five words best describe your personality? How about your best friend's personality? Whatever traits you wrote down — optimistic, loyal, imaginative, determined, organized etc. — can also be revealed by a handwriting analysis.

There are dozens and dozens of possible personality traits and any one person has lots of different ones that make up their character.

Get a bunch of friends to come over and have a personality profile party! Have everyone write down a paragraph — you should use the same one you wrote earlier — and then go through the list below (which lists a lot of common traits) and see how close everyone's handwriting is to how they really are — or to how they're seen by others! Check the celebrity samples against the info below too. Keep a running list of the traits that describe you, your friends, and the celebs. A personality party can be a real hoot as long as you all have kindness as one of your personality traits!

Imagination - or, How Loopy Are You?

One of the first things you may notice about cursive writing is that there are a lot of loops in it, some above the line and some below the line. (Even if the paper has no actual lines, there are the invisible lines you created when you wrote

the words down — lines that the writing "sits" on - that we call baselines.)
Loops above and below the baseline tell us a lot about imagination.

Imagination means much more than making up fanciful stories or
picturing yourself as the latest pop star. There are several different kinds
of imaginative thinking that you'll find below. And they're all revealed in
two "zones" in your handwriting: the upper zone (loops above the
baseline) and the lower zone (loops below the baseline).

Material Imagination

Here's a simple example of material imagination at work.

It's morning and you're hungry for
breakfast. Thanks to your material
imagination you can imagine what you'd
like to eat, say a bowl of cereal with
bananas, milk, and buttered toast.
You could make your own breakfast
if you had to, once you've imagined
what it is you'd like to eat. It would be
pretty hard to get yourself fed if you
couldn't even imagine what you were

going to make. You would be standing in the kitchen for a long time doing nothing if you didn't have any material imagination at all!

But everyone has some degree of material imagination. If you don't have a very active material imagination you might know you were hungry but not think much about what you'd want to eat. You would just wander around the kitchen to see what there is and then pick something to eat.

As the name "material" suggests, this type of imagination has to do with the real, or material, world. Your degree of material imagination is revealed in your handwriting by the size of the loops below the line. Large loops are a sign of a very active material imagination. Smaller loops are a sign of a less active material imagination.

Material imagination helps you to imagine your immediate or distant future, recall the past, picture what you want, and be more creative in the present moment.

A person with a more active material imagination also craves more variety than a person with a less active material imagination. If your loops below the line are big you probably have a lot of friends that you like to do lots of different things with.

Someone whose loops are incomplete has what is called a "latent" imagination. That person may have tons of ideas but they just don't really become fully formed. So that person will not be as likely to act on those ideas. Here's an example of the latent material imagination:

(Note: "f" and "p" lower loops have special meanings that you'll learn later.)

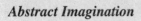

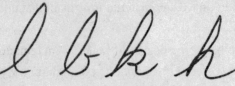

A person with an active abstract imagination has lots of ideas about things that may exist more in their mind than in the physical world.

Let's look at an example.

Krista and Nicole were excited about the opening of a big new amusement park in their city. They heard that it had lots of rides, like a Ferris wheel and roller coaster. It also had a restored steam locomotive pulling an old passenger car that you could ride. They went together on opening day and headed for the rides.

Krista immediately wanted to go on the roller coaster, and Nicole wanted to get on that old train. They flipped a coin to see what they would ride first. Nicole won the toss, so they both boarded the train. As the train pulled out of the little station and bumped and rattled along the tracks, Krista became preoccupied with the view. She could see the roller coaster from the train window and watched it plunge and spiral, until the train took her out of view. Then she passed a pretty little lake and Krista enjoyed watching some kids playing at the edge of the water. She couldn't wait to get to the roller coaster and the rest of the park, but thought that the train ride was "okay."

Nicole, on the other hand, hadn't noticed the roller coaster or the lake. She had been deep in thought since the train had left the station. She ran her hand over the old wood at the side of her seat, and imagined the people that must have ridden this very same rail car maybe a hundred years earlier. Were they immigrants heading to a new life? Did they have to leave family and friends behind? Why did trains replace the horse and wagon? Many such thoughts went through Nicole's mind as the train rumbled its way around the park and finally back to the station.

Krista and Nicole shared the same train ride — but each had a completely different experience!

Nicole, in this example, is clearly the one with the more active abstract imagination. A person with a more active abstract imagination has more of a tendency to consider many things about a thing or a situation that would not be as apparent or important to a person with a less active abstract imagination.

Which one of the two friends best describes you in the same situation? Where do your friends fall out in the above example?

Well, looking at your handwriting will reveal all. You can find out how active your abstract imagination is by checking out your upper loops. (NOTE: Don't dwell on the upper loops in the letters "f", "d", "p" and "t" here. They have special meanings all their own, as you will soon see.)

Higher, or longer upper loops mean that a person tends to be an abstract thinker. The presence of these long loops also shows a greater leaning towards a deeper level of understanding of abstract ideas than a person with shorter upper loops. The person with a more active abstract imagination is also generally more interested in the ideas of others than is the person who writes shorter loops.

Whatever loops you or your friends made, don't sweat it. You can always imagine yourself — and your handwriting — a different way!

T-rrific Goals!

Do you aim high and work hard to achieve your goals? Or, do you aim low so that it's easier to reach your goals? Bet everyone in the room has the same goal right now — finding out how your handwriting reveals your goal setting style! The cross-stroke on the lower case "t" tells a lot about what kind of goal setter you are. Let's take a look at six basic "t" cross positions.

Low "t" cross:

This person does not want to set any real goals. The most goal setting this person would do would be, for example, to catch the school bus on time that morning - a simple, immediate goal. This person doesn't spend much time thinking about the future. If you're a low "t" crosser, you're not likely, for instance, to challenge yourself to achieve good grades in subjects that are hard for you.

Medium "t" cross:

This person will set practical goals that are fairly easy to accomplish. This person wants to be sure to succeed at achieving their goals, so they have to be practical. This person thinks some about the future, but doesn't focus on striving for anything difficult. An average or passing grade in a tough subject seems like a practical goal to this person.

High "t" cross (near the top of the stem):

A "t" crossed near the top of the stem reveals a person who is confident in their ability to reach high goals.

This person is still practical about their achievements. A high "t" crosser will always try to do just a little better than before, and is not afraid to push themselves a little to achieve something worthwhile, even if it takes some time.

Top "t" cross *(at the very top of the stem):*

Got your "t" crosses at the top of your "t" stems? Then you're someone who has set yourself some real challenges, but you believe in your ability to reach high. You'll work at a goal until it is achieved — no matter how long it takes.

Floating "t" cross *(above the top of the stem):*

The floating "t" cross reveals someone who really wants to achieve their goals, but just doesn't know how. This type of goal-setter hopes others can help them figure out how and where to start. This person generally doesn't set very practical goals and therefore has a hard time achieving them.

Faint Floating "t" cross *(light stroke above the top of the stem):*

This trait looks similar to the floating t-cross described above, except that the cross-stroke is very light compared to the stem of the "t".

This faint floating "t" reveals a person who would be described as an extreme daydreamer - someone who really feels the urge to escape the daily grind by dealing more with fantasy than reality. This person finds it more difficult to accomplish things outside of their own fantasy world.

Finding this to be weighty stuff? Well, the weight of the "t" cross also reveals things about you and your goals!

Weight of the t-cross (heaviness of the stroke):

t t t

The position of the "t" cross tells about the kinds of goals you set, but the weight, or heaviness, of the "t" cross stroke tells just how much will-power or determination you have to accomplish your goals. The heavier the stroke, the greater your inner determination to accomplish whatever type of goal you set.

The "t" is turning out to be a very intense letter, with every stroke revealing something about you and your goals. Even the height of your "t" stem tells a little story.

Height of the "t" stem:

top top top

The height of the "t" stem tells us how far into the future your goals reach. A short "t" stem means that you set immediate here-and-now goals. A longer "t" stem indicates more concern for future goals and accomplishments.

Mixed Goal Characteristics:

title

The characteristics described above reveal basic types of goal-setting personalities. But in reality, your handwriting shows a mix of these traits. That's just fine, because we're not always consistent about our goals.

Sometimes we set high goals, and consider our future, and other times we may do just the opposite! And there are a lot of different possible combinations. For instance, you could set high goals (high "t" cross), but only for the present (short "t" stem). Or, you could set practical goals (middle "t" cross) that take you well into the future (long "t" stems).

So do any of the combinations suit you and your friends to a "t"?! How'd the celebrities do? You know they're all high achievers with big goals, but do their signatures reveal that too?

Determination — When The Going Gets Tough

You have seen how the weight of the "t" cross shows the degree of determination to accomplish goals. But there is another sign of determination found in handwriting, and it is a little different in meaning than the weight of the "t" cross.

g y

This stroke is called a descender — the downstroke below the baseline - in lower case "g" and "y".

A long stroke reveals a strong determination to succeed even if things get tough along the way.

Persistence — Hanging in There!

Let's say someone writes long descenders in their lower case "g" and "y". That person is determined to succeed at whatever goal level, no matter how rough it gets. But if it stays rough for a while will they be able to hang in there?

The ability to hang in there no matter what — to be persistent over time — is revealed by the presence of persistence knots. Those knots may be found in many different letters, like "t", "q" and "f".

Stubbornness

Stubbornness may seem like persistence, but it's not the same. The difference between the two is that persistence helps you to overcome obstacles that get in the way of your goals, while stubbornness may stop you from giving up a lost cause and trying something else. A tip-off to a stubborn streak in handwriting is in the tent shape, or open stem, of the letter "t".

Holding On To What You've Got

A person who has tenacity will strive very hard to hold onto the things they have, whether it's material possessions, friends, ideas, beliefs, etc. Hooks at the end of a stroke show tenacity.

The size of the hook indicates the importance of the thing that the person is being tenacious about. The larger the hook, the greater the attachment to the person, thing or idea.

Just Gotta Have It!

chave

Practically everyone wants to acquire something at some point — a new sweater, a new bike, a new CD. In its extreme form "acquisition fever" can be called "greed." If this compulsion is a really a part of a person's character, the "gotta-have-it" trait will likely be revealed by a hook at the beginning of a word.

Initiative — and Seizing an Opportunity

initiative

Has anyone ever said to you, "Go ahead, take the initiative!" when there was something you wanted to do but for whatever reason you just couldn't get started? Sometimes initiative — taking that first step —   is easier than at other times. In handwriting, upstrokes that have   steeper angles than the rest of the writing in general, are a sign of an initiative-taker.

You have to really look closely to recognize initiative angles.

The tendency to recognize and act on opportunity is revealed in handwriting by breakaway or v-type strokes in the lower case "g", "j" and "y". The greater the breakaway angle, the stronger the desire to seize an opportunity.

  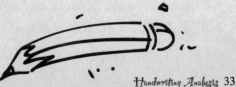

Way to Go!

d stems

Almost everyone appreciates a pat on the back. It's great to be told that you did a good job cleaning up your room, that your wrote a good paper, that you wore a cool outfit, etc. Being praised can actually make you motivated to do more. So, if you're not getting your just kudos from others, do you ever find yourself patting yourself on your own back? It's okay to admit that; most people do it at least some of the time.

The height of the stem in the "d" reveals the degree of the desire for the approval of others. The higher the stem, the greater the desire for approval.

The difference between desire for approval and self-approval is sometimes difficult to see because self-approval is also revealed by the height of the "d" stem. With self-approval, those "d" stems are extremely high in comparison to the rest of the writing. (An extremely tall "t" can add support to the tall "d" self-approval trait.)

Handling Criticism

Criticism can be tough to take. Of course it depends in part on how the criticism is being dished out. How sensitive you are to criticism is revealed by the loops in your lower case "d" and "t" stems. The wider the loops, the more sensitive you are to criticism.

Since loops in writing also have to do with the imagination, you can see how very wide loops in the "d" and "t" stems would reveal an individual whose imagination makes the criticism seem even worse!

A good rule of thumb would be to criticize others the way in which you would prefer to receive a criticism yourself — no matter how wide anyone's loops are!

Self Confidence

You and I.

The trait of self-confidence is revealed in handwriting by large capital letters, in particular the personal pronoun — capital "I".

Showmanship - or Time Robber ?

Have you got a flair for being showy? Your handwriting can reveal that quite easily. Check out how much your letters are embellished, especially those capital letters. It can also be a sign of a time waster. Which trait the embellished letters reveal may depend on the situation.. How showy are the writing samples of your celebrities?

How showy are the writing samples of your celebrities?

Making Decisions

decisive

How decisive are you? How long does it take you to decide what toppings you want on your pizza? What television show to watch?

If you have no trouble making decisions, and can pretty much do so without help, then you are decidedly decisive. Your handwriting will support that by showing firm ending strokes.

If you're undecided about how decisive you are, then you are probably at least a bit indecisive. It's hard for you to eliminate options and just pick a direction or a thing. If you question the decision you finally do make, then you fall into the indecisive category.

Still not sure if you're indecisive? Check out the ending strokes in your handwriting. If they're weak — if they taper off and are lighter than the rest of the writing in general — then you are decidedly indecisive. (But you may decide to change that!)

indecisive

Organization

Are you well organized? How are you doing keeping track of your personality profile and those of your celebs? If you see well-balanced upper and lower "f" loop extensions in your handwriting, then you do have some special organizational ability.

P is for Physical

Do you like flexing those muscles — running, bike riding, swimming, dancing, walking? How physical a person you are is revealed by how full the loop is in your lower case "p". A fuller loop indicates a more physical person. Many athletes have very full "p" loops.

Who's got the widest "p" loops in your group? Make them run and get you all some sodas!

Physical Precision

Okay, — not to make anyone with wide "p" loops feel like there's something missing from their way of doing things — but there is a difference between enjoying being on-the-go and being precise about it — having a sense of timing and/or rhythm. Narrow or retraced lower "p" loops are an indication of physical precision, rhythm and timing. In general, the writing of a physically precise person (a three "p" person?!) will also reveal extra care in the formation of letters.

Procrastination

Procrastination. Surely that's a word you've all heard in relation to homework! And to helping with the dishes! There are certain things everyone just drags their heels about doing once in a while. The small "t" cross and the small "i" dot reveal how much of a procrastinator you are.   The further to the left that the "t" cross or the "i" dot is placed, the stronger the trait of procrastination.   (After you're done with this book, you may procrastinate about ever writing anything ever again!)

Half Full or Half Empty

An optimist will look at a glass that is filled up to the mid point with water and declare that the glass is half full. This is taking a positive look at the glass. A pessimist, on the other hand, will say the glass is half empty. This is more of a negative outlook.

Think you know where you fit there? Well, your handwriting will tell you just that. Your degree of optimism is reflected by the upward slant in your "t" cross; the upward slope of your words, and the upward slope of sentences on a page.

t slope

The upward slope of sentences is not the best way to judge optimism. This slope can only be seen if your writing was made on unlined paper, since you would follow the lines on lined paper. Also, the slope may be due to having the paper at an unusual angle. It's better to look more at the slope of your "t" cross, and the slope of individual words to determine the trait of optimism.

The trait of pessimism is revealed by a down-slope in your words and sentences.

sloping down

Again, it's better for you to look at the down-slope of individual words to determine the trait of pessimism than at the down-slope of sentences.

Self-Consciousness

m n

How do you feel about being in that last school play? Did you just cringe at the thought of being on stage with everyone watching? Do you hate speaking up in class because you're afraid you don't know what you're talking about? Are you having trouble sharing your personality profile with your friends right now?

If you're self-conscious it'll be revealed in your handwriting by an increase in the height of successive strokes above the base line. Don't worry, you can get over being self-conscious-it can get easier. And then your handwriting won't be so increasingly tall!

Concentration

she skipped along

Do you find your mind wandering off in class? Or can you stay focused? How do you do at that card game where you're supposed to turn over cards to find pairs? Can you concentrate enough to remember where the matching cards are?

The concentration trait is revealed by smaller than normal letters. The smaller your letters, the greater your ability to concentrate.

Larger than normal writing indicates a lack of concentration.

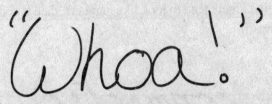

"Whoa!"

People with this trait will be more able to consider many things in general, but will find it more difficult to focus very intently on any one thing.

Manual Dexterity

n m n

Are you good at building things? How are you at games like cat's cradle? Can you juggle three apples at a time? Manual or physical dexterity (good physical control and manipulation of hands) is revealed in many flat-topped structures in your handwriting, as in the example above.

Attention to Detail

i j

Attention to detail is revealed by the placement of the "i" dot or the "j" dot close to the letter.

Math Aptitude

small 3, 7, 2, 6

If your handwriting is small, you make simple number formations and your capital letters tend to look like numbers, then it adds up that you are good at math!

Logic

connected

Very legible writing with all the letters connected, and a left-leaning d-stem loop, reveals very orderly thinking.

Intuition

I definately sense

Intuition - what you know to be true in your gut — is revealed in handwriting by a stick-like capital "I" (personal pronoun) and some disconnected letters, all made using light pressure.

Inventiveness

Just Say No!

Inventiveness (ingenuity) is a type of creative material imagination. In addition to the lower "loops of imagination," you will see printed capitals, some non-connected letters, and some originality in the writing.

Good Memory

yes, it comes to mind

Do you remember things easily? Don't worry if you can't remember whether or not you do. Your handwriting will reveal it for you! If you do have a good memory your handwriting will show long beginning strokes, fairly heavy pressure, and all "i" dots and commas consistently in place.

Cautiousness

look before you leap .

If you tend to be on the cautious side, your handwriting will support that by having very long final strokes at the end of lines.

Extrovert / Introvert

very outgoing

Are some of your friends more outgoing than others? Are some extremely outgoing? Well, those friends may be extroverts. If they are, their handwriting will be large and legible and filled with open "o" letters.

Your introverted friends — who tend to keep more things inside than most folks — will have handwriting that features a back-flung "t" cross, generally in combination with a vertical writing slant.

Egotism

Who among you has a very high opinion of themselves and isn't shy about showing it? Well, even that person's handwriting reveals their egotism with very exaggerated capital letters.

Argumentative

Which of your friends is going to head up the debate team someday? Who's the lawyer-in-training in the group? Your "p" stems will tell all. When the top of the "p" stem is higher than the following "p" loop, the writer tends to be argumentative.

patience

Patience is revealed in handwriting by consistently round, centered "i" dots, and light pressure.

Impatience is shown by "i" dots to the right, with wide letter spacing in mostly illegible writing.

Humor / Sarcasm

Do you have the ability to laugh at yourself and not take certain things too much to heart? A sense of humor - the ability to rise above doom and gloom and keep perspective — can get you through some tense spots and some tough situations.

Humor is revealed in handwriting by a curving stroke, called a flourish, at the beginning of some letters, and is especially noticeable in many capital letters - for example, "M", "N", "W", "P" and sometimes "T", "t" and "F".

The more pronounced or exaggerated the flourish, the stronger the trait.

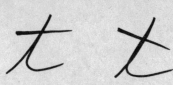

Then, there is the trait of sarcasm. You may think that sarcasm is a form of humor; after all, it's often disguised in an apparently funny remark. But don't be misled - sarcastic remarks are not meant to be kind. They make fun of people in a hurtful way.

Sarcasm is revealed in handwriting by a "t" cross that is a heavy stroke that ends with a point.

If that "t" cross is also angled down, it is showing a tendency to dominate others.

Assertiveness

This trait shows up in handwriting as a downward slanting "t" cross, but, unlike the domineering "t" cross, this person makes a point without having a domineering point on the end.

Jealousy

Jealousy is revealed in handwriting by a flattened right-to-left stroke finished with a left-to-right curve — a loop with a flattened bottom — most often in capital letters at the beginning of a word.

Bet you won't be jealous of someone who's got that stroke in their handwriting!

What makes your blood just boil? How good are you at keeping your cool? If you lose it easily, your handwriting will show that you have a very heavy "t" cross stroke to the right of the stem. The farther the cross stroke is to the right, the greater your lack of temper control. Now don't get mad at that!

Worry

We see the trait of chronic worry revealed by upside-down loops in the writing. (Don't take it too seriously if your loops are upside down — you could just turn the paper around, no?!)

Pride

Very large capital and other letters, and a very wide left margin on the page, taken together, are indicators of a sense of pride.

Exaggeration

Extremely full, exaggerated loops indicate a tendency toward exaggeration in the writer. If seen in upper loops, ideas and beliefs tend to be over-blown. If found in the lower loops, the writer tends to be a teller of some tall tales!

Loyalty

Want to find out how loyal someone really is? Check out the "i" dots — if they're carefully rounded as opposed to streaky or dash-style dots, then you have a pal you can count on through thick or thin.

Desire for Attention / Center of Attention

Do you like that spotlight? Know someone who just craves being the center of attention all the time?

A much stronger than normal desire for attention may be seen in tall final strokes on words - taller than the height of the tallest letters in the writing, and may be supported by tall "t" stems.

tall finals

A center-of-attention trait is revealed in handwriting by a special addition to the writing — a big, round happy-face, a heart-shape, or some other attention-grabber. You might see it as a replacement for the "i" dot, and often as part of a signature.

Generosity / Stinginess

generous.

The trait of generosity is revealed in handwriting as an up-curved final stroke, and may be supported by an openness in the writing and wide page margin on the right.

(How generous you're being to your friends by letting them see what their handwriting reveals about their personalities!)

Stinginess is the opposite of generosity. It is normally revealed by "squeezed" handwriting.

Secretiveness

loops

The trait of secretiveness is revealed in handwriting by closing loops on the right side of circle letters or structures. The larger the loop, the more significant this trait.

Resentment

this

A rigid upstroke starting below the base line of the writing reveals the trait of resentment. Try and let it go! You can do it!

Irritability

the

Do things just bug you sometimes? Everyone gets cranky on occasion. This funky feeling is revealed in handwriting by a long, pointed "t" cross supported by angular writing with "ticks" or small hooks.

Reliability

I will help Bob .

This trait is revealed in handwriting by very even-sized letters, unwavering sentences, and a capital "I" (personal pronoun) not larger than other capitals.

Versatility

A a g g 9

The trait of versatility is revealed in handwriting by a mix of written and printed styles of capital letters and a wide mix of different letter styles. It may also be supported by varying slants.

Sincerity

I really mean it .

Unwavering sentences and some simplified letter forms, reveal sincerity as a trait - and may be supported by a right slant.

Tactfulness / Tactlessness

You tried hard .

Decreasing letter size with some disconnected letters reveals tact.

Increasing letter size and wide-open "o" letters reveals tactlessness.

you lose .

Diplomacy

diplomatic

Diplomacy (skill in handling "sticky" situations) is revealed in handwriting by thread-like word endings, decreasing letter size and closed "o" letters.

Open or Closed Minded?

Are you an especially open-minded kind of person? If so, your handwriting will feature a full, fat "e" and very rounded circle letters "a," "o," "d," "g," "q."

e a o d g q - e

If, on the other hand, you're especially closed-minded, your writing will show a poor little squeezed "e" instead of a nice full and rounded one.

A normal-looking "e" indicates that neither trait rules.

So how did you do? What traits are on your list? What have you learned about yourself and your friends from your handwriting? Were there any big surprises? Any disagreements? How did the celebrities wind up? What traits do you have on their lists?

Bet you never realized how complex — and how individual — everyone is. There are loads of different personality traits that go along with an emotional base and way of thinking. No two individual's handwritings are exactly the same — and that's because no two people are!

Chapter Five
All Together Now!

You've gotten so much information about yourself from the last three chapters — you've discovered how responsive you are to things, how deeply you feel things, how you approach problem solving, and what list of traits best describes your unique "youness". Now it's time to put it all together and form a more complete picture of who you really are. If your list of personality traits includes some things you'd rather not have on it, don't despair. Maybe the degree to which you feel these things is very light. You need to see how all the things you've learned fit together.

Check out the two examples below. They'll give you a sense of how to do the same thing with all the stuff you've found out about yourself.

These samples come from two sisters: Amanda, who's eleven, and Megan, who's thirteen. Even though they're sisters, their personalities, interests and ways of expressing themselves are really very different from one another — as you can see from their very different handwriting styles. Pay particular attention to the weight of the writing, the size of the letter formations, and the slant of the upstrokes. Those characteristics will give you the big picture on each of the girls. See how many other characteristics you can find in their writing!

Personality Picture One: Amanda (11 yrs. old)

(weight of Amanda's writing: moderately heavy)

Upon a horse
Upon a horse, I feel fearless + strong
The wind flapping through my hair
I focese on the road that's there
The hoofs pounding on the ground
I can't beleive how fast I went around
Upon a horse I feel strong inside
My heart swells up with pride
The horse flaps his tail at the flies in the air
I stap him to say good samenare
Up on a horse, I feel fearless + strong
Just intel someting goes wrong
He speeds up uncontrollably
I yell "Whoa" and pulls on the reins
And because I forgot to grab a handful of
mane,
I am in the durtin pan
Up on a horse, I feel fearless + strong
Just until someting goes wrong

by
[signature]

Even if you couldn't tell from her handwriting that Amanda, the younger of the two sisters, is an extremely creative and imaginative person, you'd know it just by reading her terrific poem!

You can tell that even though Amanda's emotions run deep (as you can see from the weight of her writing) - and that certainly helps where her creative and artistic expression is concerned - she also has a lot of emotional reserve about her (check out the straight up and left-slanted upstroke angles).

At this point in her life, Amanda's self-confidence wavers, though this is masked by a generously sensitive and caring nature (note the combination of the varying size of capital letters, heavy writing, and the wide left page margin).

Amanda is an abstract and cumulative thinker (revealed by the long, full upper loops and broad, flat "r" tops) - there's a lot of wonderful stuff going on in her head, but she often finds it difficult to focus or concentrate long enough to see things through to a proper finish (indicated by the large size of her letter formations). This is supported by a cautious and not very optimistic nature (see some long final stokes and also note the down-slope to the writing). Perhaps this is why Amanda's goals are often set far below her abilities and potential (note the many low "t" crosses on long stems).

But there are signs that Amanda wants to assert herself and to show the world what she's made of (long, up-slanted "t" crosses). Her need for approval stretches to self-approval (tall "d" stems) and this, combined with strong emotional and creative/artistic energy (in the weight of the writing and in the long, full loops), caring sensitivity to others (combination of heavy writing and wide left margins), and her ability to look ahead and consider her future (those long "t" stems), will help Amanda to discover how much she has to offer.

Personality Picture Two: Megan (13 yrs. old)

(weight of the writing: heavy)

> Kim shuffled down the sidewalk, adjusting her backpack on her shoulders. She kicked a pebble and listened to it click so against the sidewalk. She sighed and walked into the ravine. She hummed a tune as she skipped along the gravel path.
>
> Kim stopped dead in her tracks and sniffed the air. There was a new scent... a strange scent wafting between the trees. Kim cautiously stepped into the fringe of trees. Pushing aside a tree branch, Kim peered into the shadows. What she saw made her recoil in silent horror.
>
> Megan Vanalstine

Megan, the older of the two sisters, is a heavy writer. And, like her sister, Megan is not always willing to draw upon that deep well of emotional energy.

In contrast to her sister Amanda, Megan is a little more organized, and a lot more focused (note the more balanced "f," small letter size, and the absence of a on the page). Most of the time, she can concentrate on her schoolwork and other things that interest her. And most of her focus is on the concerns of the here-and-now (check out those short "t" stems and low and short "t" crosses). In addition, Megan can sometimes be very responsive, which she projects to others (occasional strong right slant of the upstrokes).

Again, you could tell not only from her writing but also from the content of her sample that Megan is also very creative (remember the loops of imagination?), though in a different way than Amanda. Megan is more analytical and logical than her sister, but she is not as much of an abstract thinker (as seen in shorter, smaller upper loops and, some left-leaning "d" stems). She is more concerned with the "nuts and bolts" of things, and is a little more materialistic than philosophical (short, small upper loop).

At this point in Megan's life, she is not willing to set goals for herself beyond very practical immediate needs, and she also tends to under value her own abilities and potential (those low "t" crosses).

Megan's personality is super-charged with an emotional energy and intensity (the combination of heavy writing and small letter size) that, when harnessed, will drive her on to great things!

Here again you have been presented with a very rich sample in Megan's handwriting. Think about the differences between these two wonderful, talented and creative sisters, and how each of them can be positive influences on the other. That's one great thing about having a brother or a sister.

You should be ready to put all your own info together into a personality profile now. Once you've taken a shot at it, check out the next chapter to learn more about signatures. If you have been checking out the celebrity signatures introduced earlier, this next chapter will give you even more to work with.

Ready to put all your own info together into a personality profile? Once you've done yours, try and do one for each of the celebrities whose handwriting you also analyzed as you went through this book.

Chapter Six

The Public You and The Private You — or — Signing Off!

Think you've gotten Britney's personality down-pat from analyzing her signature? Is there anything you don't know now about Jim Carrey? Well it turns out that there is a difference between analyzing the body of someone's handwriting and their signature. Actually, a signature cannot by itself be used to completely reveal a personality, because it is not a large enough sample of a person's handwriting. Don't worry, though. The analyses you did were a cool way to practice your newfound skills and should reveal some interesting traits.

You know, a signature can also reveal something a little different about the writer's personality than the body of writing.

Check this out. The body of your handwriting tends to reveal the private, or natural you. It shows how you think, feel and respond to other people and to circumstances, and how you tend to deal with life — all the stuff you just found out about yourself.

Your signature, on the other hand, shows more of how you want to be seen or understood by others. It is more of what you project to the world — your signature is really a kind of showcase into which you put some of the things you want others to notice about you. Even though you write automatically, without thinking about what you're doing, when you sign your name to something, you are actually more conscious of it than you are about your normal writing. When you write your signature, your mind creates more the public "picture" of yourself that you want to project.

Right now you might not see much of a difference between the paragraph you wrote and your signature. As you get older, though, your signature will probably change more from the body of your writing. Your writing will change as you grow anyway, but your signature will most probably branch off even more as you mature Ask your best friend or Dad to write a paragraph and sign it to see if that's true for their handwriting. (Then keep the samples and see if you can build a personality profile for them!)

The most complete analysis of a person's handwriting that you could do, then, would include a signature so that you could compare the private and the more public sides of that person.

To find out what "face" you're showing to the world, compare your signature to the examples below.

In addition to what you have already learned about handwriting, here are some of the special kinds of things that signatures may reveal:

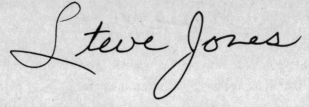

That forward slash in the "S" tells us that Steve is especially proud of his accomplishments, and he wants you to know it.

This Steve is not too comfortable being a "Jones", as indicated by the decreased size of that last name.

Here, Steve is particularly attached to his middle name, as evidenced by the pronounced "B". He would have written "Bartholomew" in full, but it's a tad too long for a signature!

Definitely no lack of self-confidence in Steve here, as indicated by the underscored name, ending with a stroke to the right.

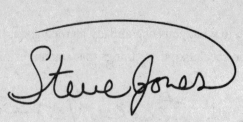

Steve Jones

This Steve is quite extremely concerned with his own well-being, as shown by the protective back-slash over the name.

Alicia,
this is for you.
— Steve

Our writing, and our signatures, can even reveal how we feel about another person. When Alicia got this note from Steve, she could have known from the exaggerated size of her name, "Alicia", that Steve really likes her a lot - and isn't afraid to show it!

Steve,
Thanks, but I don't
need it !
Alicia

On the other hand, Steve could have known by the relatively small size of his name in this reply, that Alicia would prefer it if Steve was on another planet.

Have you gotten any notes lately?

Did you see anything in the above examples that's in your own signature? Do you now have another piece of the puzzle that is "you" to add to what you already know?

Let's take a look again at the samples we analyzed in the last chapter, this time focusing instead on the included signatures, to see what Amanda's and Megan's signature tells us, and how those signatures compare to the body of their writing.

Handwriting & Signature Sample One: Amanda

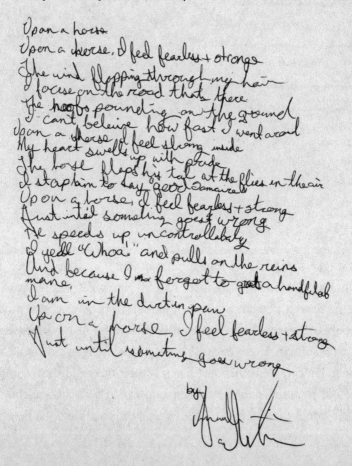

Well, there are clearly some differences between Amanda's normal writing and her signature! She really wants others to see her as the special, creative and sensitive individual she truly is. She will find a way to stand out in a crowd, and will appear to be more confident than she actually feels - but, true to the nature revealed in her normal writing — she will be extremely cautious about where, when and how she does it. One thing we can be sure of is that Amanda will find very imaginative ways to stand up and be noticed!

Handwriting & Signature Sample Two: Megan

Kim shuffled down the sidewalk, adjusting her backpack on her shoulders. She kicked a pebble and listened to it click so against the sidewalk. She sighed and walked into the ravine. She hummed a tune as she skipped along the gravel path.

Kim stopped dead in her tracks and sniffed the air. There was a new scent... a strange scent wafting between the trees. Kim cautiously stepped into the fringe of trees. Pushing aside a tree branch, Kim peered into the shadows. What she saw made her recoil in silent horror.

Megan Vanalstine

Megan's signature appears remarkably similar to her normal handwriting. We could say that, with Megan, what you see is what you get - there won't be any apparent contradictions between the private and the public Megan. You can count on her to be just as intense, and as unpredictable, in either case (besides, sometimes "predictable" can be boring, can't it?). Unlike her sister, Megan doesn't feel a strong desire to be the center of public attention, and would be a little uncomfortable or even annoyed with the demands that it might place upon her.

Of course, with both of these signatures, as with the handwriting in general, there is more there for you to discover. Give it a go, and see what you can add to these analyses!

And finally, let's see how close you got to building accurate personality descriptions for the celebrities in this book, based upon their signatures. Don't be too hard on yourself if your trait descriptions aren't too long — after all, you were only working with their signatures and not the body of their writing. It's mainly the more public sides of their personalities that they have shown you here.

So grab your notes now and see if we came to some of the same conclusions about the more public sides of these popular celebrities:

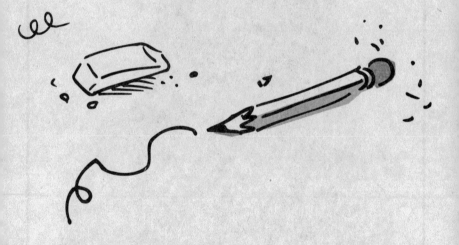

Britney Spears

Britney's signature tells us that she is not only extremely comfortable performing on stage or in her music videos, but that she is actually more confident on stage than she is away from the public eye. She really needs you to show her how much you appreciate her talent. So go ahead — tell her how much you love her!

Jim Carrey

Jim Carrey plays larger-than-life, over-the-edge personalities — but he wants you to know that, underneath it all, he is really a shy guy (believe it or not !) who is more comfortable keeping to himself when he's not performing. But give him all the praise you can for his performance — he'll eat it up!

Wayne Gretzky

"The Great One" is certainly one of Hockey's greatest stars of all time. His signature says he's serious about being really good at what he's done, on the ice and off. Wayne Gretzky has a lot of interests besides hockey, and he takes the initiative in all of his pursuits — he's a leader, not a follower.

Jessica Simpson

As confident as Jessica is when performing, this singer is still on a search to establish her own unique identity both as a performer and as a private person. That means, if you're following her career, you may be in for some surprises! Her signature says "Like what I've done? Well, you ain't seen nothin' yet!"

Jennifer Lopez

Jennifer Lopez sings, acts, models and that's probably just the beginning of her exploration of her many talents. But she wants you to know that she's not just a driven entertainer, she's also a thinking, caring and passionate individual.

N'Sync

Here's Justin, Chris, Joey, Lance and JC. Take a look at their signatures and see if what you think you know about these talented guys is "N'Sync" with what their signatures tell you!

With this book as a guide, and with more practice, you'll be able to learn more about your friends, family, teachers, and anyone else whose handwriting you come across.

So, keep on doing the write thing! 🙂